30 Days of Hope for Single Moms

Hope that renews energy, vision, and life

Lois M. Breit

Copyright © 2018 Lois M. Breit

ISBN: 978-0-9887398-3-3

Editing by Sarah R. Young

Formating by Pamela Beaudry

Cover by Vicki Higgins/Higgins Design

All scripture quotations are from the New Living
Translation (NLT), New International Version (NIV), or
Message (MSG).

Printed in the United States of America

Dedicated to:
Doug, Peter, Jill, Ben, and Pamela

—you always encourage and inspire me.

The stories shared in this devotional are true, but the names have been changed.

INTRODUCTION

I wrote this devotional book to encourage and restore hope to all women, but especially single mothers. Whether you've lost hope because of a rebellious child, health issue, or the loss of a job, home, or loved one —The God of Hope desires to *"fill you with all joy and peace . . . and an overflowing hope."*

I chose several topics in this book that challenge us as women and moms. Life can seem overwhelming in the moment—but God always offers us hope! Some of the daily topics may seem insignificant, however, trying to find safe childcare or affordable transportation to work becomes a major stress when your job and means of support are in the balance.

I pray you are drawn closer to God, *the source of hope*, as you read these scriptures, take the daily challenges, and witness the testimonies of God's faithfulness.

May the God of hope fill you with all joy and peace as you trust in him, so that you may overflow with hope by the power of the Holy Spirit.

Romans 15:13 (NIV)

Table of Contents

Day 1

Hope Lost — *Find It*

May the God of hope fill you with all joy and peace as you trust in him, so that you may overflow with hope by the power of the Holy Spirit.
—*Romans 15:13 (NIV)*

Hope deferred makes the heart sick, but a longing fulfilled is a tree of life.
—*Proverbs 13:12 (NIV)*

Most women, at some point in life, will experience a bout of hopelessness. However, as single moms, we can suffer long periods of hopelessness because we've given up on ourselves, our kids, or on God. We don't believe we can change things, we feel helpless—we become hopeless! We think God has forgotten us, is mad at us, or just doesn't care.

We need God, and the power of the Holy Spirit to have our hope restored. Hope is restored when we quit looking at our circumstance, when we let go of what was—or what happened—and begin to look at possibilities again. Proverbs 13:12 says, "A longing fulfilled is a tree of life." Our energy is renewed and joy returns when we have something to look forward to again, a new longing (hope) to replace what has been lost.

You may not know what the future holds, but if you trust in the Lord, He promises to fulfill your longings. Does that mean we get whatever we want? No. But it does mean He will restore our joy and peace and set us on a new path toward new opportunities. The longer you sit and feel sorry for yourself, rehearse your defeats, or complain about others, the longer you'll remain trapped in hopelessness and be heartsick.

How do you find hope when you're feeling hopeless? Go to the source of hope—God. Read scriptures that will develop faith and renew your hope in life. Praise and worship God, even when you don't feel like it.

Today: Don't try to tackle everything, but choose just one thing that's making you feel hopeless today. Ask God to bring you relief and the help you need— just for today. It helps if you have a friend whose life is in balance or a counselor to walk through this time with you.

●●●●●●

Jennifer was hopeless after her husband died. Her will to live waivered, her children suddenly became a burden instead of a joy. Her grief was only deepening. Then she went to a retreat for single moms and realized she wasn't alone in her emotions. She wasn't going crazy. She heard words of hope and the other women surrounded her with their strength. Sometimes we need each other—we can't find that illusive hope on our own. We need the right people with the right attitudes to pull us out of ourselves and draw us closer to God where we find hope again.

2
Day

Hope for a Career — *Change It*

Your word is a lamp for my feet, a light on my path. —Psalm 119:105 (NLT)

You may not know what career path you want to follow, you may feel stuck in your job, or you may have had a dream of a career, but that dream seems to be changing. God often takes us on different career paths throughout our lives—you don't have to consider just one career for life.

The disciple Peter thought he would be a fisherman his entire life: God made him a "fisher of men" as an evangelist and church leader.

The apostle Paul was a proud scholar and educator. He could have had any position he desired, but God made him a tentmaker who traveled as a nomad, planting churches across the nations.

Luke was a doctor, Matthew a tax collector, Mary a prostitute, yet God had a seeming impossible new direction for each of them. They set off into their unknown "careers," trusting God for something they could not yet see. They did not allow fear of the unknown or fear of failure stop them.

God may have something new and unusual for you, or He may keep you right on track where you are. Just be willing to follow His lead, whether it's to hold steady, take a promotion, or change careers.

When you feel stuck in a job you hate, one that doesn't meet your financial needs, or just isn't you—it may be time to seek godly advice.

Today: Write down your dream jobs—don't limit yourself to one. Ask yourself if you're allowing God to "light your path" or if you're just taking the path you landed on. Gather information on how to attain your dream job or begin to take steps in your current job that will prepare you for promotions.

• • • • • •

I had training as a secretary and administrative worker, but when I was broken and hopeless, God lead me to a church where I became a janitor, then a secretary, and then an associate pastor. Later God set me on another new career path as a missionary and writer for single moms. I was afraid and felt unqualified for most of these new paths. However, I knew God was leading me. He was the light when it seemed dark and unknown. He took away my fears— and there were many—as I walked out the steps. God continues to grow and change us when we're willing to hear His voice and follow His lead.

Tina had worked at a fast food chain for years. They offered to promote her to manager several times, but fear of failure caused her to turn down every offer. She remained stuck in a job that didn't meet her financial needs, chipped away at her self-confidence, and stopped her growth toward new opportunities because she listened to the voice of fear instead of the word of God.

3
Day

Hope for Childcare — *Research it*

All your children will be taught by the Lord, and great will be their peace. —*Isaiah 54:13 (NIV)*

God wants you to have peace about who watches your children and how they will be taught, and He wants your home to be at peace.

Finding the right childcare is the most important goal of every working mother. It's never easy to leave your children in the care of someone else, and budget restraints can make this choice even more difficult.

It takes time to research qualified daycare providers, but doing your homework pays off. Find the centers or caretakers you can afford, then ask as many questions as possible. Talk to other parents. Don't be shy—this is for your child's safety.

Pray hard about your choice. Pray for your child each day before you drop them off. Listen to what they say about their care and activities. If there's something they don't feel comfortable about, find out why.

Teach your children about inappropriate touches. Teach them proper names for their body parts so they can accurately describe where they've been touched.

Even preschoolers have a sense of right and wrong touch and behaviors. Teach them that keeping secrets from you is not okay and no one should ever ask them to do so.

Leaving your child with someone else can be the hardest thing any mother has to do, and you want no regrets in this area of parenting. For the shy and non-confronting parent, don't be afraid to change providers if need be.

Today: Research providers and their costs. Choose ones you can afford. Tomorrow begin to gather references from neighbors or other parents using the center.

• • • • • •

Barb had her child in a home daycare for over a year. One day her four-year-old daughter began to cry when she went to drop her off. She asked what was wrong and her daughter said she didn't like when Mr. _____ was there because he always wanted to tickle her and she didn't like it. Barb immediately took her child out of that daycare, pursued the comments of her daughter, and the dad was eventually found guilty of molesting several of the children in that center. Don't live in fear, but be wise and diligent and listen to your child.

4
Day

Hope for Cooking — *Savor It*

She is like a merchant ship; she brings her food from afar. She gets up before dawn to prepare breakfast for her household and plan the day's work for her servant girls. —*Proverbs 31:14–15 (NLT)*

Ever stress or just give up trying to decide what to fix for dinner? How often do you stop at your favorite (or the most affordable) fast food restaurant just to avoid cooking? And why is it we keep forgetting to take something out of the freezer in the morning that we can cook for dinner that night? Easy answer: we're tired!

Meal planning and preparation can be just plain monotonous. Cooking is one more chore added to an already very busy, hectic schedule, yet it's an important one. It's not easy to stretch your dollars to feed your family—it takes planning, budgeting, and smart shopping skills. However, once you get the process down, cooking at home is not so bad.

Here are a few easy tips that may give you hope for healthy, happy meal times:

1. Write out a daily meal plan that coincides with your paycheck. It might be weekly, bi-weekly, or even monthly. Take your time, think it through, make it fun. Involve your kids by asking for their input. Go online and research quick easy meals—there are many!

2. Write out your grocery list to match the meals you've planned. If you're on a tight budget, cut the junk foods that keep you from cooking (chips, soda, frozen meals with extremely high sodium).

3.Whenever possible, make two meals in one night—the one you're going to eat that night and one for the following day. Crockpot meals are the easiest.

These are just a few starter ideas. I'm sure you can come up with more ideas of your own. The main point is to take the pressure off daily meal planning and cooking. Let cooking become something you do together as a family, or your own personal quiet time while the kids do homework, watch TV, or play.

One more tip: eat together without the TV on, and put phones away. Meal times are the best opportunity for families to bond, converse, and relax. You'll be amazed how your kids will begin to talk when you prepare the right atmosphere.

Today: I challenge you to make a food budget if you don't already have one. Then work on a meal plan for your next pay period. This may take time to establish, but once you do, meals will become a joy instead *of* something that bring you to the breaking point. You don't have to be the perfect Proverbs 31 woman, but without goals, you'll remain overwhelmed and hopeless.

• • • • • •

When my husband left, I cried every day and meals were the last thing on my mind, but I eventually had to let my responsibilities toward my family override my own grief. I gradually began practicing some of the things listed above so we didn't eat the same "easy" meal several times a week. To this day, my now-grown kids still hate the word "goulash"! You'll feel less hopeless when you're eating healthy and mealtimes are a gathering place instead of a free-for-all.

5
Day

Hope for Family — *Believe It*

. . . "Sirs, what must I do to be saved?" They replied, "Believe in the Lord Jesus, and you will be saved—you and your household." —Acts 16:30–31 (NIV)

Have you been praying for a family member? You know Jesus could change their life, but they just don't seem to listen? Acts 16:30–31 gives us the simplicity of salvation along with a hope for those we love.

This is the story of a jailer who was guarding Paul and Silas in prison. As they sang songs of praise to God, an earthquake struck. All of the prisoners could have walked out, and the jailer would have been killed for allowing them to escape. However, when the jailer awoke, he saw Paul and Silas were still sitting there. This miracle led the jailer to faith that day, but the disciples wanted him to know his entire family could have the same salvation.

The jailer brought them into his house and set a meal before them; he was filled with joy because he had come to believe in God—<u>he and his whole household.</u> —Acts 16:34

The jailer's family made the decision to come, to stay,

to listen, and to choose to believe. They were given the *opportunity* for salvation because of his faith.

In Acts 10:24–47, both Peter and Cornelius were given a vision in order to break the cultural barriers that *separated them*. When Cornelius heard the hope found in Jesus, He chose to accept Christ as His Savior. It opened the door for his family to also hear and choose to follow Jesus for themselves.

When we come to Christ, our prayers, words, actions, and faith all move our family into a *position of opportunity*, and then choice. They may not all *choose* to follow, but they will be given the opportunity.

Today: Have you accepted Jesus as your Lord and Savior? If not, it only takes a simple prayer of faith to ask for forgiveness and invite Jesus into your life. Hope for your family is real because of your choice to follow Jesus. Living out your faith daily, gives them the opportunity to hear and believe for themselves.

• • • • • •

Mikkie was a volunteer at an event for single moms. It took a lot of coaxing for her to convince her angry, resentful, and estranged single mom to attend the event. Because Mikkie gave her mother the opportunity to hear, receive, and respond at this retreat, her mother found Jesus. She accepted Him as her savior, found freedom from her anger, and immediately began to reconcile with her daughter. Mikkie later said, "This was the first time I got to pray with my mom instead of for my mom." Their relationship has continued to heal and grow as her mother walks out her new-found faith and freedom.

Don't give up on your family. Prayers do impact and open doors of opportunity. Sometimes God uses you, and other times He uses outside influences to speak to your family members. We can't force anyone to come to Christ—our faith does not guarantee theirs—but we can set the stage for them to hear and accept the Gospel because of our faith.

6
Day

Hope for Custody — *Pray for it*

Those who fear the Lord are secure; He will be a refuge for their children. —Proverbs 14:26 (NLT)

Fear and worry over the custody of your children may be one of the biggest battles you will have to face. I cannot guarantee the fate of a child's custody, but I can guarantee God will never leave them (or you). I've seen unfair custody outcomes, and I've seen miracle outcomes. If you're in a battle today, don't lose hope! Pray hard, stay close the Lord, and live your life with integrity regardless of how others act—and regardless of the outcome.

I lived under the threat of a custody battle I felt hopeless to win. I prayed night and day and surrounded myself with people who built my confidence and drew me closer to God. My court battle never came—the threats were only hollow—but I found my strength in Christ when I had no strength of my own. God was my refuge!

If you've lost a custody battle, don't lose hope! If it was an unfair judgment, continue to pray and set a good example for your children. Bitterness will destroy you and drive your children further away. If your choices caused the judgment, don't lose hope!

Begin to make better choices, seek wise counsel, and change your lifestyle. Your children deserve the best you can be.

I've seen the courts return children to parents who have proven their lifestyle and attitudes have changed. Surround yourself with people who will teach and help you, not those who keep you down. God is a God of restoration, and He has a new plan for your future, whether you can see it or not. Stay close to Him during your defeats, and He will restore your hope and your future.

Today: If you're facing a custody (or visitation) issue, find at least one person to pray for you. Pray for God's protection over your children and that He will be their refuge (safe place), wherever they may be. Then find your rest as you hope in Christ to do what you cannot.

• • • • • •

Lisa cried at the altar at a retreat one night. She had lost custody of her children to her lawyer ex-husband. He had the resources and power to fight and win the battle. She was devastated, defeated, and hopeless. Lisa needed to find a strength she didn't posses, a will to live that no longer existed, and vision for a life she didn't want. As Lisa surrendered her grief and loss to the Lord, she *"experienced God's peace, which exceeds anything we can understand"* (Philippians 4:7a).

Lisa found hope as she embraced God's love. Her grief and anger began to subside throughout the retreat. She experienced God's peace and strength and realized it was not only for her, but also to help her children through the months or years they would not have her at their side.

We cannot stay parked in the "Why God?," "It's not fair!," or "God has forsaken me" parking spaces. We may never know why, but we must accept life isn't fair and believe God is always with us, even when we feel defeated.

Never give up hope, moms, even if you've lost a custody battle. Keep praying and moving forward! Your kids will become adults one day soon and will see things through different eyes. How do you want them to see and remember you?

7
Day

Hope for Fierceness — *Strengthen It*

For God has not given us a spirit of fear and timidity, but of power, love, and self-discipline.
—2 Timothy 1:7 (NLT)

When I talk about fierceness, I don't want you to confuse it with a rude, know-it-all behavior. Fierceness is an acknowledgment of your value, belief that your voice matters, and a determination to follow through on issues that matter to you.

I once watched a Hallmark Channel movie called *Love's Complicated.* It was about a nice woman who wanted to make everybody happy, even at the cost of her own happiness. Her boyfriend signed her up for a conflict management class, and when she arrived, she realized he wasn't coming. Throughout the movie, I watched a kind-hearted woman struggle to speak up for herself, trust her own judgments, and in the end, find her voice. She wasn't rude, arrogant, or judgmental, she just became fierce (strong) in the knowledge of who she was and what she wanted. I related to this woman so much that every time I see it on the schedule, I watch it again.

Fierceness is confident, relentless, full of fire—the opposite is weakness, benign, ineffectual. As women we can be kind, yet fierce—determined to survive, unafraid to speak our minds, and able to give strength to our families. I'm still pretty shy, but something rises up inside me when I know I need to speak up for myself or someone else. Finding a balance can be hard when you're moving from a fear-driven or doormat position to finally managing your life with the fierceness of a confident, Christ-like attitude.

Today: Start your journey to fierceness by believing you have value and your voice matters. Think of one cause that deserves fierceness. It may be for your child, it may be for yourself. It could be job related or family related. Write it down! Get advice if needed, and work at becoming fierce—confident and determined!

• • • • • •

I spent years letting other people make decisions for me. When they'd ask where I wanted to eat or if I wanted to go somewhere, I always responded with "I'm fine with whatever you want." I ate at restaurants I didn't like, went to movies I didn't want to see, and even listened to gossip I didn't want to hear.

But God continued to use 2 Timothy 1:7 to remind me that He didn't give me a Spirit of timidity (fear), but of power, love, and a sound mind (self-discipline). I had no hope for fierceness until I realized my feelings and choices were just as important as others' feelings and choices. It doesn't mean I should always get my way or be rude, but I shouldn't be afraid to speak up, either.

Fierceness comes as our confidence builds. It's a strength that comes from within. The Spirit of God is power, love, and a sound mind, and His Spirit gives me the confidence to be me.

8
Day

Hope for Finances — *Break It*

Dishonest money dwindles away, but whoever gathers money little by little makes it grow. — Proverbs 13:11 (NIV)

I lay the sins of the parents upon their children; the entire family is affected—even children in the third and fourth generations of those who reject me. But I lavish unfailing love for a thousand generations on those who love me and obey my commands. — Exodus 20:5b–6 (NLT)

These scriptures talk about two aspects of our finances. The first passage is about integrity and hard work. The second passage is about rejecting God and the effects it has to the third and fourth generation. But what do they mean for you today, especially regarding your finances?

Proverbs 13:1 speaks to the fact that we must work hard to gradually make our financial situation change. There is *hope,* even if you can't see it at the moment. It takes time, vision, and often furthering your education to little by little make your money grow. Quick money is rarely honest or realistic.

Exodus 20:5 talks about the "sins" of the parents visiting to the third and fourth generation. This is not because God hates you, but because there are consequences to our choices, and because we pass on our habits and attitudes to our children. However, God gives us *hope* through Jesus, who offers us forgiveness and a new beginning—even in the face of poverty.

Exodus 20:6 says, *"He will lavish unfailing love for those that follow Him."* Repentance (turning away) from sinful lifestyles and a decision to follow Christ are what breaks the destructive and generational patterns in our family. When you choose to live for Christ, you may not become rich, but you can begin to make wise and healthy financial choices. This is a heritage you can pass on to your children!

If you're currently on welfare to sustain your family, look at ways to become independent of it so you're not trapped in poverty or a limited financial future (seek out a financial counselor). Discover your passion and work toward it. Get your GED, continue your education, get trained in retail, or find a job that gives you the opportunity to excel. Many a cashier has become a manager by being a responsible, dependable, hard-working employee.

Don't believe you will always be poor. Your hope is renewed little by little as you become responsible for what you have and then break old poverty attitudes and habits.

Today: Believe in yourself. Find hope in God's ability to open financial doors that have been closed in the past. Start to dream again! Set one new financial goal, no matter how small—or big—it may seem. You can break the cycle of poverty in your family by making new choices today and in the future.

• • • • • •

I took two major steps, years apart, to help set me free from a poverty mentality and lifestyle. First, I took a job that put me less than $10 over the maximum I could earn without losing my welfare benefits. Food stamps gone! Medical for my kids gone! Monthly stipend gone! I could have stayed home, not worked at all, and earned just as much. However, by accepting that new job, I was set free to follow God wherever He would lead me. If I'd stayed on welfare, my income would have dwindled as my kids aged out. I'd be stuck in poverty forever! Instead, I was free to increase my knowledge and skills and advance to better jobs. (Welfare was a life saver, but I didn't want it to become a lifestyle to be passed on to my children. If you are unable to set yourself free, find a path for your children to break the cycle.)

My second breakthrough came when my son wanted to go to college and I said we couldn't afford the school he wanted to attend. But again, we prayed, applied for every scholarship, grant, and non-loan funding we could find. (I didn't want him buried in debt when he graduated.) Research opened many doors to grants we hadn't known existed. He had a job and worked hard all through college, and he made it through with only one small loan his last year. Because he broke the cycle, the rest of his siblings had hope for a college education, and they, too, went on to attend and graduate college.

It's time to hope for the impossible when it comes to your finances and just see what God may do for you!

9
Day

Hope with a Disability — *Prevail in It*

Yet God has made everything beautiful for its own time. He has planted eternity in the human heart, but even so, people cannot see the whole scope of God's work from beginning to end.
—Ecclesiastes 3:11 (NLT)

But Moses pleaded with the Lord, "O Lord, I'm not very good with words. I never have been, and I'm not now, even though you have spoken to me. I get tongue-tied, and my words get tangled."
—Exodus 4:10 (NLT)

But when the people of Israel cried out to the Lord for help, the Lord again raised up a rescuer to save them. His name was Ehud son of Gera, a left-handed man of the tribe of Benjamin . . . —Judges 3:15 (NLT)

. . . Therefore in order keep me from becoming conceited, I was given a thorn in my flesh, a messenger from Satan to torment me.
—2 Corinthians 12:7b (NLT)

"Pardon me, my lord," Gideon replied, "but how can I save Israel? My clan is the weakest in Manasseh, and I am the least in my family." —Judges 6:15 (NIV)

These are stories of men who had disabilities of one kind or another. God has always cared about, and mightily used, those who others see as weak or cast-offs.

Many scholars believe Moses stuttered, yet he was called to be God's voice to Pharaoh and to the Israelites.

Ehud was left-handed. This was considered a defect, even a curse, and he was seen as someone without value. Yet God chose him—*because* of his disability—to get past the guards to kill the king and free the Israelites.

It's believed Paul had issues with his eyes, but regardless of the disability, he preached the Gospel and brought hope and salvation to the Gentile (non-believing) nations. He did all this *while suffering* with the disability of a "thorn in his flesh."

Lastly, we look at Gideon. God used a man who was the *weakest of the weakest* to save a nation! Note that, in verse 12, God calls Gideon a mighty warrior before he even climbs out of his hiding place because God sees what we cannot.

The world sees a disabilty, while the Lord focuses on the strengths He put into each of us.

Living with your own disability, or with your child's, is never easy. However, God encourages us with these stories of resolve, favor, boldness, endurance, and strength while dealing with a disability.

You and your child will influence others throughout your lifetime. Many people may find their own hope because your family exhibits love, strength, smiles, and faithfulness in the midst of real struggles.

Today: Begin a search for your own emotional and physical help and relief. You'll need breaks and the wisdom of others to be the best mom—and person— possible. You may never know the "why", but you can prevail knowing God has a plan for you as well as your child. Don't lose hope in the midst of exhaustion. Remember, prevail means to become dominant, win out, prove superior strength, influence. Take a deep breath and start fresh today.

• • • • • •

James had cerebral palsy. He was in a wheelchair for most of his life. His mother abandoned him to his grandparents to raise. The physical challenges grew as James moved into his upper teens and his grandparents into their 70s. Even while he grew bigger and they grew weaker, they never complained. They only loved James more. James was part of youth activities even though he was hard to transport and his speech was hard to understand. James and his grandparents' love and courage impacted so many lives. The grace of God gave them the ability to spread joy and hope to others who were facing thier own personal crisis. They prevailed with love and joy in a situation they could not change or control.

10
Day

Hope for Guilt — *Defeat It*

For God did not send his Son into the world to condemn the world, but to save the world through Him. —John 3:17 (NIV)

Did you wake up feeling guilty about something again today? Did you say or do something to deserve that guilt? Have you asked for forgiveness but continue to be buffeted with guilt?

Today is the day to be released from guilt and condemnation. Guilt keeps you trapped in your past, and self-condemnation steals your future. There are a few easy steps to get over guilt.

First, determine if your guilt is justified. Did you actually do something that deserves guilt, or has someone just made you feel guilty? If you did something, apologize if possible, and ask for God's forgiveness. Then let it go. You cannot undo words or actions, but don't allow them to steal your joy.

If your past haunts you but you've asked God to forgive you, it's time to accept His forgiveness and move on.

You'll stay in bondage to guilt until you choose to accept the forgiveness God offers you. Remember our opening scripture: God did not come to condemn the world (you), but to save the world through Him. That's the hope we have—we no longer need to live in guilt day after day. We've been set free!

Today: Seek forgiveness wherever needed. If you've asked for God's forgiveness, accept it! Say this out loud: "I'm forgiven. It's over. I refuse to live with guilt. I'm moving forward."

• • • • • •

The biggest guilt I struggled with for a long time was the failure of my marriage. I would think of all the things I should have, or could have, done differently. I felt my children suffered without their dad because I had failed as a wife. I know I wasn't perfect and never will be, but it also took me a very long time to believe I wasn't a horrible person and the entire cause for the failure of our marriage. Their dad made a choice that affected all of us—a choice I didn't want, couldn't stop, and had no control over. But I still felt guilty. It stole all my joy, all my ambition, and all my hopes. Thankfully, I was set free from guilt and condemnation when I accepted God's forgiveness for my sins and let go of the sins of others.

11
Day

Hope for Life — *Choose It*

Today I have given you the choice between life and death, between blessings and curses. Now I call on heaven and earth to witness the choice you make. Oh, that you would choose life, so that you and your descendants might live! You can make this choice by loving the LORD your God, obeying him, and committing yourself firmly to him. This is the key to your life. —Deuteronomy 30:19–20a (NLT)

Sometimes your circumstances are so overwhelming, or you're so extremely tired of fighting battles, that you just want to give up. Suicidal thoughts can make their way into your mind until death sounds much easier and more inviting than the daily battle of life
.

However, God wants us to choose life. He wants to bless us and our children with a new future, but we must make the choice to live, even when it's hard.

This scripture tells you how to choose life. *Love the Lord*, regardless of your situation—He didn't cause it, but He will help you get through it. Obey Him by studying His Word so that you can respond to it. *Commit yourself fully to Him* by following after Christ with all your heart and soul. Don't allow others to get you off track and into the dark place of depression.

Surround yourself with people who encourage you, challenge you, love you, and teach you. Get involved with *life, the living, and avoid isolation.* Verse 20a says, "This is the key to life."

Why choose life for yourself? So "your descendants might live as well." The act of suicide affects the entire family for the rest of their lives. I know—I've seen the aftermath of suicide and what it does to the children, siblings, and parents of the person who chose death over life. It's causes endless grief, guilt, anger, and feelings of abandonment.

Choose life, and you'll be surprised what God does when you give Him the chance to restore and heal the brokenness of today and make it into something beautiful tomorrow. He really does!

Today: If you're struggling with suicidal thoughts, get help. Talk to a doctor, a pastor, or a friend. Do not ignore the symptoms of isolation, on-going sadness, thoughts of death, mood swings, or self-destructive habits. If just facing your daily responsibilities is pulling you down, find a way to get a break. This is why the church family is important. They can often step in and help—when they know the need. Don't let independence, shame, and fear stop you from asking for help!

• • • • • •

Jessica met with me about four years after I'd preached a message at her church. She told me how she had come that morning with her suicide planned out. She wouldn't have come that Sunday, but she'd already promised to bring a friend to hear me. But that Sunday was meant for Jessica! Hearing a message of hope, life, and possibilities saved her life. She left with new thoughts and a new hope. She met with her pastor and found the relief she needed and the counseling and encouragement that helped her find a new job. She told me how God spoke life into her that Sunday morning

.

Do not give up on life, moms! God is the giver of life—if you learn to love Him—even in the midst of your mess!

12
Day

Hope for Health — *Care for It*

Dear friend, I hope all is well with you and that you are as healthy in body as you are strong in spirit.
—3 John 1:2 (NLT)

When we're struggling with health issues, it affects everything. Whether it's a serious illness, the flu, being overweight, or some other issue, it can be debilitating. When you've lost hope in so many things, an added illness can be the last straw.

Remember today, as you seek to become closer to God, your spirit is being strengthened. As your spirit is strengthened, your thoughts become more rational and less emotionally driven. Then the body often responds in a positive manner.

Do what you can to improve your health. Make better food choices, exercise, go to bed and get the sleep you need. When there's nothing you can do to change your health issue, pray! Pray for healing, wisdom, help, the right doctors, and for God's peace in the midst of it all.

Stop asking why—that question just keeps you stuck in depression, guilt, shame, anger, and resentment. We usually never know the why, only that God is our strength when we're at our weakest. After Paul asked repeatedly for the "thorn in his flesh" to be removed God answered: *"But he said to me, 'My grace is sufficient for you, for my power is made perfect in weakness.'"* —2 Corinthians 12:9 (NLT)

Today: If you're feeling weak or ill, ask for God's grace to get you through. If you're able to change your condition, take one first step toward a better health choice. If your health is out of your hands, keep your eyes on Jesus for your daily strength and put on a worship CD to encourage your spirit.

• • • • • •

Amy had constant migraines that interrupted her work and ability to care for her children. She tried many things, but one day decided to give up caffeine. It changed her life. The migraines stopped, she was able to function again, and she has not suffered since. She's often tempted to have "just a little" caffeine but is reminded of the agony it causes. This may not be the answer to all migraines, but Amy took a difficult step to give up something she loved and enjoyed in order to care for her health.

Jane had breast cancer. She went through major surgeries to remove her breasts. She was a single mom, and her friends prayed fervently for her to survive when the doctors gave little hope. It was a terrible year for her, and I'll never know why she had to suffer so—but Jane's faith never waivered. She actually built my faith as I watched her react to the continuous negative reports from the doctor. Today she's healthy and active again. When we face a health issue bigger than us, the biggest battle we often fight is in our mind. Jane's faith conquered that battle, and she had hope throughout her entire ordeal.

13
Day

Hope for Joy — *Rejoice in It*

He sets the time for weeping and the time for joy, the time for mourning and the time for dancing. —Ecclesiastes 3:4 (NIV)

Then I will hold my head high above my enemies who surround me. At his sanctuary I will offer sacrifices with shouts of joy, singing and praising the Lord with music. —Psalm 27:6 (NLT)

When tears don't stop flowing, heartache never seems to end, and sadness is worn like a warm coat, it's hard to believe there will ever be a time of joy again.

Believing God is not the cause our hurt, and that He actually wants to help us through those times, can change everything. You can begin to believe the hurt will eventually stop, even if you don't know how or when. You can begin to believe the sun will shine again in your life, even if you can't feel it today.

Joy can't be forced. Pretending doesn't fool people for long, either. Joy must be real. How do you get it back? Time, prayer, and most of all, worship. By singing songs of praise, even when you least feel like it, something unexplainable happens within you. Our spirits communicate with the Spirit of God through our praise and worship. We're changed from the inside out through worship. It focuses our minds on the goodness and glory of God instead of our problems. Songs from scripture give us hope and remind us of God's promises for good days. Your problems may not go away, but your sacrifice of praise (Hebrews 13:15) renews hope.

Today: Turn on your radio, listen to iTunes, or play a CD that lifts you up and makes you smile. Sing along. See if it doesn't begin to make a difference. I can't say how it does, it just does. That's God.

• • • • • •

I remember crying myself to sleep more nights than I care to think about. I also woke up many mornings feeling depressed or sad. But I also know that when I began to praise God for what I had, instead of dwelling on what I didn't, I was changed. Music full of hope and promise made the difference, and I was surprised by joy.

14
Day

Hope for Justice — *Seek It*

He has shown you, oh man, what is good. And what does the Lord require of you? To act justly and to love mercy and to walk humbly with your God. —Micah 6:8 (NIV)

Cursed is anyone who denies justice to foreigners, orphans, or widows. — Deuteronomy 27:19 (NLT)

Have you been wrongly accused of something, or maybe many things? Do you fear a court appearance? Have you lost your children due to no fault of your own? Have you become hopeless that justice will ever be served in your family?

God brings justice when you put your trust in Him. It may take longer than what you like, it may not look the way you expect, but God's justice is always just (Deuteronomy 27:19)!

Don't give up praying. It builds your faith. Even when you feel let down, God does hear! When you fear the Lord, you understand His power and ability to do what you cannot.

Keep moving forward with your own life, regardless of your accusers or your losses. It will not be easy, but God honors those who honor Him. Every day is the right day for you to do the right thing. You can't control what others will do, but you also won't be judged by God for their actions, only your own.

The Israelites were seeking forgiveness, searching for atonement (a price) for their sin in Micah 6:8. God tells them to do what is right, show mercy (even when things are unfair), and walk humbly before God (because we continuously need his forgiveness as well).

Today: Find hope for justice by living your life in an honorable way. Replace one bad response today with one that will honor God instead. Show mercy when you only want to express anger. Allow Him to bring justice in His time and His way. Embrace the fact you cannot change others, pronounce judgment, or make life fair.

• • • • • •

Laura came to the altar crying one night after a single moms event. Her husband had moved in with her sister, right across the street from her. How do you ever find justice in that? Laura couldn't, and I didn't have words that could help her live with that pain. But I could pray with her. We prayed for God to be the judge of that situation, to give Laura the words to explain to her children that their new cousin would also be their half brother. Life just isn't fair, and Laura could only find peace when she gave her painful circumstance to Jesus. Without Him, she would have no hope for justice or peace. Not all stories have a happy ending, but people can find peace even in the midst of injustice. Laura left that retreat a different, stronger woman. Even though her circumstance hadn't changed, Laura had!

I didn't share a story of great victory because sometimes God's judgment takes longer than we like. But judgment day will come! I don't even know the outcome of Laura's story, but I do know she and her children will be rewarded and blessed for their actions—and not face the judgment of God—as they *act justly, love mercy, and walk humbly with their God.*

15
Day

Hope for Legacy — *Develop It*

"And this is my covenant with them," says the LORD. "My Spirit will not leave them, and neither will these words I have given you. They will be on your lips and on the lips of your children and your children's children forever. I, the LORD, have spoken!" —*Isaiah 59:21 (NLT)*

Most single moms live below the poverty level, and the thought of leaving their children an inheritance is foreign to them. But all moms can leave their children a legacy.

A legacy is "anything handed down from the past, as from an ancestor or predecessor." What was handed down to you from your parents or grandparents? Was it good or was it bad?

The Spirit himself testifies with our spirit that we are God's children. Now if we are children, then we are heirs—heirs of God and co-heirs with Christ, if indeed we share in his sufferings in order that we may also share in his glory. —*Romans 8:16–17 (NIV)*

With God as our Father, we a have the ability to leave our children a wonderful legacy. We can break past legacies and habits and develop new ones with our choices and actions. Our kids can always choose the wrong things, but our responsibility is to leave them a good legacy.

Here are just a few examples of a good legacy: kindness, compassion, strength, independence, integrity, faith, and financial responsibility. We can also leave a legacy not influenced by drugs, alcohol, or abuse.

If you received a good legacy, pass it on. If your legacy was poor, or your life has left you empty, don't give up. God gives us hope for our children because we are His children and heirs to His blessings. Learn those blessings by reading the Word and then pass them on to your children!

Today: Make a list of the poor family traits (the legacy) you were left with. Now crumple it up, and throw it away. That legacy is no longer a part of who you are in Christ! Then make a list of what legacy of faith and life you want to leave for your children. Ask yourself who's around you who can help you build a new legacy for your family. Can't think of anybody? Then get to church, my friend!

• • • • • •

My parents weren't rich—they weren't even Christians. However, they left my sister and I a legacy of honesty, responsibility, vision, and compassion. They weren't affectionate, but we knew we were loved. They didn't go to church, but they made sure we did until we were old enough to decide our own beliefs.

They sheltered us from family and friends who could cause us emotional or physical harm. They were strong but treated people with respect. They taught us "you can," not "you can't," and they left us a legacy of opportunity! I could list a hundred things I wish they had done differently, but I'd rather be thankful for the many things they got right, and the rich legacy they left us.

16
Day

Hope for Better Days — *Restore It*

And the Lord says, "I will give you back what you lost to the swarming locusts, the hopping locusts, the stripping locusts, and the cutting locusts. It was I who sent this great destroying army against you. [Even in the midst of rebellion, God wants to offer restoration]. Once again you will have all the food you want, and you will praise the Lord your God, who does these miracles for you."
—*Joel 2:25–26 (NLT)*

You may be wondering how you'll ever get your life under control again, and if the darkness will ever pass. This verse was given to a decimated Israelite nation to give them hope for a better day. They had rejected God, they were being disobedient, but God still loved them and wanted to restore them. Joel 2 lists the blessings awaiting them, whenever they chose to return to Him.

This scripture is a reminder of God's promise to both the life-long Christian who has become weary and the new Christian who has yet to hear these words of hope. Remember, God desires to restore your brokenness, pain, and losses. He promises better days ahead when our hope is placed in Him. God is the God of hope, so by nature, He offers us hope for better days.

Restoration is a wonderful word of hope. The dictionary describes it as the act of restoring; renewal, revival, or reestablishment. How we got where we are is a thing of the past. If you need to repent (turn away from sin or poor choices), do so. If someone else has caused your problems, let go of your anger and give that person(s) to God to deal with. God can't build something new on a pile of burning embers (anger or hatred). We need a new, clean, solid foundation to start the rebuilding process.

The Israelites had to think and act differently before restoration could take place. Restoration takes time, patience, and a changed attitude or outlook on our part.

Today: Believe restoration is possible! Stop blaming others. Seek forgiveness yourself. Smile at least once today because you have put your hope in God to fulfill his promise of restoration. Better days are ahead!

• • • • • •

God could not start my restoration process until I quit crying about my life, my mistakes, the choices others had made, and the unfairness of life. Once I took the step to put my hope in Him and His way, not mine, my restoration process started and better days did come!

17
Day

Hope for Love — *Expand It*

And I will give you a new heart, and I will put a new spirit in you. I will take out your stony, stubborn heart and give you a tender, responsive heart.
—Ezekiel 36:26 (NLT)

Three things will last forever: faith, hope, and love—and the greatest of these is love. —1 Corinthians 13:13 (NLT, see also MSG) Trust steadily in God, hope unswervingly, love extravagantly, and the best of the three is love.

Do you feel you'll never be loved again? Discouraged in your loneliness? Hopeless?

Well, I can't guarantee you'll find Mr. Wonderful and live happily ever, but I can tell you love is not your enemy or your savior. Love in today's culture tends to mean sex, and it's generally self-fulfilling rather than other focused. But that's not God's definition. Ezekiel says love has to do with the condition of our heart— compassion, tender, thinking of others. The book of 1 Corinthians reminds us that faith, hope, and love last forever.

Your faith, hope, and love for God will keep you centered in all of your relationships—friends, family, and men. Also, you cannot fully love if you have a heart of stone (walls), have lost tenderness (responding to the needs of others), or have a non-responsive heart (unable to hope for love, not just sex). If you don't grasp God's love, it's almost impossible to succeed in earthly love.

God's love is not earned, it's unconditional. This means God dearly loves you always and forever, no matter your past. There's nothing you have to do to earn that love or even keep it—God loves you just the way you are today! Nothing can separate you from His love (Romans 8:39 says, *"indeed, nothing in all creation will ever be able to separate us from the love of God that is revealed in Christ Jesus our Lord"*). You can reject God's love, but He will still love you. If you reject His love, you will also miss the blessings that come with it.

It's God's love that heals our pain, draws us out of isolation, and moves us to love others. Loving our neighbors, coworkers, and even the difficult people around us becomes easier when we know we are loved.

Avoid steps toward a romantic relationship until you first find contentment in your singleness. This will prepare you for a much healthier relationship based on mutual giving, not a one-way or needy relationship.

Being single doesn't mean you're without value or are unlovable. You actually have more opportunities to love God, pursue your dreams, and set new goals.

If you're ready to pursue romance, be sure your children are also ready. You want to avoid, at all costs, choosing between a man you've fallen in love with and having a good relationship with your children. Be choosy, be wise, take your time, protect your children, seek advice from solid friends *and* listen to them!

Today: Be thankful for God's love. You don't have to work at earning it, you just need to accept it. Then think of one act of kindness (love) you can extend to someone else today.

• • • • • •

I vowed to close my heart to love after my husband left. I never wanted to go through such great pain and loss ever again. Shutting people out became much easier, and isolation much more comfortable. One day I realized what I had done to myself. I was dead inside, hope was gone, life was gone, and I only existed to care for my children.

When I finally accepted the love God had for me, everything changed. My hope in life was renewed, and joy replaced the endless grief I'd been living in. It was God, not a man, who opened my heart to love and removed my loneliness.

Hope for Peace — *Rest in It*

Don't worry about anything; instead, pray about everything. Tell God what you need, and thank him for all he has done. Then you will experience God's peace, which exceeds anything we can understand. His peace will guard your hearts and minds as you live in Christ Jesus. —Philippians 4:6–7 (NLT)

What is peace? Have you experienced it lately? That place where your mind isn't racing, trying to solve every problem, tackle every worry, or fret about every need? Peace is a hard thing to hope for when you're a single mom carrying all the responsibility for your family, but it can be found!

Have you prayed about these problems, believing God will answer? We may pray but often doubt He hears us anymore. We've lost hope for answers or peace.

Have you thanked Him for what you already have? A roof over your head, children who love you, friends, family—there must be at least one thing you can be thankful for today!

I believe when we focus on the good, no matter how small it may seem, peace follows. When we let go of our timetables, agendas, and solutions, peace follows.

When we believe God loves us and wants to bless us, He overrides our fears and anxieties and brings us peace.

Almost every letter of the New Testament was opened with a greeting of "peace be with you." That peace meant "be blessed." God wants to bless us, but sometimes we're so busy worrying that we miss His greeting of peace and miss out on the blessing.

All our worry and anxiety won't change a thing, but when we begin to trust God, our faith brings *God's peace, which exceeds anything we can understand.*

Today: Take a deep breath. Know what you can change and what you can't. Choose just one of your worries and give it to God in prayer today. Then choose not to worry about it all day. Let God take care of it! (Remember, you can't fix it anyway.) Begin to hope for peace in one area today.

• • • • • •

I once prayed with a friend who was facing surgery. She was worried she may not survive. We read scriptures to give her an assurance of salvation, we took communion together, and we prayed for God to replace all of her fears with peace. I reminded her God would be standing right next to her as the doctors prepared her, He would bring all of her vitals in order before surgery, and He would be with her throughout the surgery. She still didn't know what the outcome would be, but she had received God's peace days before the surgery, and it stayed with her throughout.

19
Day

Hope for Possibilities — *Dream It*

Jesus looked at them intently and said, "Humanly speaking, it is impossible. But with God everything is possible." —Mark 10:27 (NLT)

For the word of God will never fail.
—Luke 1:37 (NLT)

What impossible task are you facing today? What impossible future do you hope for?

Do you find yourself often saying, "I can't do it," "It's too hard," "That will never happen," or "I give up"? Those words of defeat steal a little bit of life from you each day. They'll keep you trapped in your circumstance. But how do you break free of those words when they seem to be the truth?

Read our scripture verses again. Humanly speaking, it's impossible—we can't meet our daily challenges alone. But with God, everything is possible! That's a game changer. You, I, we, can't do many things without the strength, wisdom, and power of God. Humanly speaking we're limited, but God is not!

God is creative—just look at the variety of fish, birds and animals he's created! He created each of us individually, creatively, beautifully in His eyes. We're creative beings because His creative nature is in each of us. That means we were made to dream and imagine possibilities. We just often forget to include God in our dreams.

Is your impossible dream for just enough energy to get through this day? Wisdom for a rebellious child? The right words for an ex-spouse? The courage to get your GED or take your first college course? Look for a new job? Whatever impossible task you're facing today, face it with God, not alone. Don't be afraid to hope for the seemingly impossible.

Don't stop dreaming, even in the midst of hard days. God promises to give us hope, and Luke 1:37 is a reminder of God's faithfulness to fulfill His Word!

Today: Invite God into today's challenges. Ask Him to intervene on your behalf, to go before you, to give you favor. With God, *all things are possible*. Believe it, say it, and hope for it!

• • • • • •

When I was in the middle of just surviving each day, I felt I had no "wins." I began to expect bad reports from my kids' school, stressful calls from my ex, sassy kids, a car repair, a broken water pipe, a backed up toilet, stormy weather for a planned event. A good day seemed impossible.

I would pray every day for God's help, but expected only bad things. I didn't want to hope because expectation could only bring deeper disappointment.

One day I wondered why I prayed at all, since I didn't trust God to answer my prayers. I was always preparing for the worst. I remember the day that changed. I had a doctor appointment I was worried about. I prayed and then I wrote down on a piece of paper, "I expect a good report." Every time I began to worry, I looked at that paper and spoke those words out loud. I refused to expect a bad report. I had finally tired of expecting the worst the world had to offer and began hoping for the best God had—new possibilities, for me and for my kids.

Disappointment will always be with us because life isn't fair or perfect. But without hope for possibilities, life becomes impossibly dead.

20
Day

Hope for Protection — *Prioritze It*

Have mercy on me, O God, have mercy! I look to you for protection. I will hide beneath the shadow of your wings until the danger passes by. —Psalm 57:1 (NLT)

We all have a desire to feel protected. If you've lived in a place of danger or threats, you know the importance of being protected.

There are choices we can make that help protect us, but some things are just out of our control. Those are the times we need to say out loud, "God have mercy. Protect me from this person, storm, or danger that I'm facing. *I will stay close to you, until this danger passes.*" Then stay close to Him, don't just say the words and go your own way.

The way we stay close is through prayer, reading faith-building scriptures, listening to worship music, and surrounding ourselves with other praying believers. Focus in on God and His power instead of the fear. Be smart in your choices, and find hope for protection through the time you spend in the presence of God.

Today: Tell God your fear, and be honest. Decide what you need to do in the physical to protect yourself. Seek help, if it's needed, through your local church, shelter, or police. Then pray hard, pray continuously, don't isolate yourself, and stay close to God.

• • • • • •

Ceci's husband left her to become a woman. She didn't know how to protect her young daughters from being hurt or emotionally traumatized by the changes they would encounter in their dad's new looks and identity.

God's protection: she found a group of women who prayed as she shared this news with her children, walked her through their questions, and continued to pray for their protection and understanding for years.

Mandy faced threats from her vindictive and abusive husband. He continuously took her to court just to drain her finances and keep her afraid and controlled.

God's protection: she was surrounded by people who stood with her through every battle and came to her home whenever her ex showed up drunk.

God protected these women in different ways, but they dared to hope for protection as they approached God with their needs and no longer hid in secrecy and shame from their friends.

21
Day

Hope for Reconciliation — *Pursue It*

Therefore, if anyone is in Christ, the new creation has come: The old has gone, the new is here. All this is from God, who reconciled us to himself through Christ and gave us the ministry of reconciliation: that God was reconciling the world to himself in Christ, not counting people's sins against them. And he has committed to us the message of reconciliation. We are therefore Christ's ambassadors, as though God were making his appeal through us.
—2 Corinthians 5:17–20 (NIV)

Reconcile means to win over to friendliness; cause to become amicable: to make compatible, to restore.

Before we knew Christ as our Lord and Savior, we were separated from Him, unable to receive His forgiveness and His blessings. But when you gave your life to Him, your old life was gone and you became new—reconciled or restored to God. He desires we reconcile with others whenever possible to win them to Christ. Not because they deserve it, but so they can be made new as well.

You may have differences with coworkers, friends, family members, or even your children, but God wants us to pursue reconciliation whenever possible.

We don't have to compromise our faith, beliefs, or safety to reconcile with someone.

If you're not sure why there's division, ask, "What have I done to offend you?" If you know the issue, apologize and ask for forgiveness. If they've offended you, have you told them why and how? Silence can be a deadly divider.

We cannot force reconciliation, but we must do our part by providing the opportunity. They may accept or decline reconciliation, but your responsibility as a believer is to genuinely offer it.

Remember, whether it's a friend, family member, or child you're seeking to reconcile with, someone has been hurt or offended. Apologize, seek forgiveness, offer forgiveness—start the process. Let them know you love them even when you disagree with their lifestyle or life choices. Swallow your pride in order to keep the door open for them to return to you and to Jesus! Keep your boundaries without making it impossible to restore the relationship.

If reconciling with an abuser, forgive so you're not bound to the past or to them, but keep your boundaries and your family protected.

Today: Think of one person you'd like to restore relationship with. Do you need to forgive them, or do they need to forgive you? Take one first step toward reconciliation this week, have patience in the process, and keep the door open.

• • • • • •

I knew a single mom who had built up such hatred toward her ex-husband that it was destroying her. After attending a retreat for single moms, she heard about God's love and forgiveness. She was completely changed that weekend (the old had gone, the new had come). She went home a different person. She told me a year later that her ex-husband couldn't understand why she was no longer so angry with him. She just told him she'd forgiven him and was praying for him to find the peace she had. They began to deal with their kids without all the strife. Reconciliation doesn't mean people will get back together, but it means they can live in harmony, without animosity being passed on to their children.

22
Day

Hope for Respect — *Earn It*

In everything set them an example by doing what is good. In your teaching show integrity, seriousness and soundness of speech that cannot be condemned, so that those who oppose you may be ashamed because they have nothing bad to say about us, as though God were making his appeal through us.
—Titus 2:7–8 (NIV)

"Honor your father and mother." This is the first commandment with a promise: If you honor your father and mother, "things will go well for you, and you will have a long life on the earth."
—Ephesians 6:2–3 (NLT)

We cannot demand respect from our children, we must earn it with more than our words. Our lifestyle will teach more than all the words we may ever use. In our first passage, Titus is teaching us to set an example for our kids to follow.

Do you respect your parents? If you had terrible parents, do you speak badly about them to your children? We are commanded by God to honor them in our speech and actions, not because they deserve it, but so we teach it. Don't lie about who they were, but don't berate them either.

Do you treat your children with respect, even when you disagree? Respecting them for who they are as people with kind, encouraging words of correction or teaching, but don't abdicate your parental role of authority.

Do you treat those in authority with respect? If not, your example demonstrates rebellion against authority. Your kids will have a hard time respecting a teacher, a boss, or laws if they do not respect authority.

Today is a new day—examine how you treat others, but don't take on guilt! When you feel anger rising or yelling on the tip of your tongue, take a minute to calm down so you avoid a ranting rage. If you're mad at your boss, church leader, or ex-spouse, think about how your words or actions will be interpreted by your children.

Respect is something earned, not demanded. Your children will be much easier to train in the ways of respect when they see you live out respect, forgiveness, and kindness toward others. Actions always speak louder than words.

Today: If you need to apologize for a behavior, do so. Do one small thing to show your child an act of respect—say something nice about their dad, the boss you've been complaining about, the church that may have hurt you, etc. Start building a lifestyle of respecting others, because we do reap what we sow.

• • • • • •

I knew a young woman who wanted to have a baby boy more than anything. When her daughter was born she was so disappointed she couldn't love her. The baby ended up in the hospital for "failure to thrive," basically love-deprived and neglected. I know this is an extreme example, but it demonstrates how much our children need us to accept who they are, respect their personalities, and train them to be good and healthy adults. Having children is not about meeting our emotional needs but about meeting the needs of our children and preparing them for a successful future. That is what earns us respect!

23
Day

Hope for Friendships — *Forge It*

Oh, the joys of those who do not follow the advice of the wicked, or stand around with sinners, or join in with mockers. But they delight in the law of the LORD, meditating on it day and night.
—Psalm 1:1–2 (NLT)

You may have a lot of friends or very few friends, but having good healthy friends is what matters. What makes them "healthy"? Healthy friends don't have destructive habits like drugs or alcohol, violent reactions, scary friends, or no friends.

Often when we're changing the direction of our lives or going after new goals, old friendships lose their allure. Some friends may not be "bad people" but no longer help you attain your goals. They may be negative, naysayers, unhappy people who do not encourage or energize you.

Today's scripture tells us about the joy we find in friendships that are not laced with wickedness (mean), sinners (living contrary to God's Word), or mockers (those who ridicule or put others down). It goes on to say friends delight in the law of the Lord, meditating on it day and night. This doesn't mean sitting around all day reading the Bible, but it means we know what pleases God and live according to that each day. This may mean changing the places you hang out, making a job change, finding a new hobby, or volunteering somewhere new.

Today: Evaluate your friendships, one by one. If you have friends who keep you down or pull you down, it may be time to separate from them. This may not be permanent but may be necessary until they can no longer influence you. Make a list of places you might find new friends, and take one step toward that goal this week.

• • • • • •

Sarcasm had become my wall of protection. I could vent safely and be angry, afraid, or insecure and use wit to avoid confrontation. But sarcasm is just veiled anger.

I fed my sarcasm with sarcastic friends. One day my son pointed out to me, in the middle of one of my sarcastic descriptions, that it wasn't nice to talk about people like that. Out of the mouth of babes! I had taught him one thing but was living another. I worked hard to overcome my fears so I could face situations and people in healthier ways. I learned honest, healthy emotional expressions, in confrontational situations, this helped me gain many new friends. I no longer drove people away, or attracted the wrong friends by my cutting sarcastic remarks.

24
Day

Hope for a Strong Heart — *Build It*

Guard your heart above all else, for it determines the course of your life. —Proverbs 4:23 (NLT)

This scripture tells us to guard our heart because it determines the course of our life. How is that possible?

Well, if you have a hard heart, you don't allow love in. If you have a deceitful heart (manipulative or lying), you can't be trusted. If you allow pornography or other sordid things into your heart, they become things you chase after. If you constantly say and believe "I can't," you won't.

How do you guard your heart? Proverbs continues:

Avoid all perverse talk; stay away from corrupt speech. Look straight ahead and fix your eyes on what lies before you. Mark out a straight path for your feet; stay on the safe path. Don't get sidetracked; keep your feet from following evil. —Proverbs 4:24–27 (NLT)

I think that scripture says it all. A strong heart is built on what we feed it.

Today: Begin to guard your heart by analyzing what you're allowing to enter it. List the things that make you strong, and those that stop you from attaining your future goals or hinder your relationships. Choose one bad "heart habit" to eliminate today.

• • • • • •

Irena had fallen into the habit of watching soap operas all day. Suddenly she wasn't happy with her life anymore. Her husband no longer measured up, her children didn't make her happy, and she didn't like her home. She was on the brink of leaving her husband and children when she realized what she was doing. She'd allowed unrealistic and miserable TV lives to bring unrest and dissatisfaction into her own life and home. Something as simple as a soap opera almost cost her the family she loved. Once the TV was turned off (and it was a hard withdrawal), she found purpose and joy in her life and family again.

Day 25

Hope for Success — *Work at It*

Commit your actions to the LORD, and your plans will succeed. —Proverbs 16:3 (NLT)

Do you want to succeed in your job or your role as a mom? Commit them to the Lord first.

Too often we go off on our own, without considering scriptures, prayer, or the Lord's will for us. It takes practice to change our thinking to put God first in our plans.

Successful Child Rearing: The Bible offers many parenting skills, including how to train, discipline, and love your children. There are also hundreds of books on raising children. Reading helps you become successful.

Success in Your Job: Do you have the job you want, or have you prayed about the job you'd like? Have you asked for God's favor and been a good employee wherever you are now? Have you sought training to advance in your current job, trusting God to open the right doors at the right time for promotions? We're often too quick to complain, blame, make excuses, and leave God out of our planning.

Success is not just monetary. God blesses us with emotional, spiritual, and family success as well—when we partner with Him.

Today: Write out the goal(s) you want to achieve. Commit them to God in prayer. Ask for his wisdom and direction. Take one first step toward success in just one goal this week.

• • • • • •

Abby wanted to be a social worker, but she was a single mom with three young boys. She had struggled through high school because of undiagnosed dyslexia and had only a GED. After accepting Jesus into her life, she made a commitment to follow Him first. This meant changing friends, attitudes, and her poor self-image. She set her career goal before the Lord and asked for His help.

Abby was able to obtain scholarships, and she worked hard for several years. She now has her college degree and has found the job of her dreams. Finding confidence and placing God first in her life also affected her relationships. Abby is now married to a wonderful man and together they work at making their blended family a success with God in the lead.

26
Day

Hope for Today — *Embrace It*

Those who live in the shelter of the Most High will find rest in the shadow of the Almighty. This I declare about the LORD: He alone is my refuge, my place of safety; he is my God, and I trust him.
—Psalm 91:1–2 (NLT)

Did you wake up feeling quite hopeless today, thinking there's nothing good in your life or completely overwhelmed by everything? Well, this scripture was written at a time of great distress to encourage us— there's a refuge and safe place where hope is found. When we learn to trust in God, we find the peace we're looking for, even in the midst of our storms.

We are pressed on every side by troubles, but we are not crushed. We are perplexed, but not driven to despair. We are hunted down, but never abandoned by God. We get knocked down, but we are not destroyed. —2 Corinthians 4:8–9 (NLT)

The Apostle Paul loved God, served God, and was preaching a message of hope as he shared these words or encouragement to the Corinthian people. Even while doing everything right, he met opposition. He felt pressed down by trouble and confused about his circumstance, but he was "not crushed," "driven to despair," or "destroyed" by "perplexing" circumstances. Why? Because he knew God never abandoned him! He was not going through it alone. He believed God would bring relief and rescue him.

Paul wanted the Corinthians to know—and God wants us to know—He is our strength and shelter when we're pressed down or feeling hopeless.

Today: Go to Him today in prayer and worship. Rest in His presence. Gather enough faith that God will give you the strength you need for today—just today.

• • • • • •

I often went to bed afraid, confused, or angry. I tried to find answers, tried to find peace, tried not to panic over meeting our needs. Years earlier I had memorized Psalm 91, and it came back to me on those nights or early mornings. I would just repeat it in my head and picture myself at rest with God covering me, protecting me, providing for me. I found my peace in the "shelter of the Most High" as I faced each day of fear and turmoil.

27
Day

Hope for Tomorrow — *Expect It*

I ask the God of glory—to make you intelligent and discerning in knowing him personally, your eyes focused and clear, so that you can see exactly what it is he is calling you to do, grasp the immensity of this glorious way of life he has for his followers, oh, the utter extravagance of his work in us who trust him—endless energy, boundless strength!
—Ephesians 1:18–19 (MSG)

If you've been struggling or feeling hopeless, read this scripture again and again. God desires a "glorious way of life, endless energy, boundless strength." These come through our faith and trust in Him.

He never promises life will be easy, but He does promise us contentment, joy, peace, and a future we may not see yet, but one that He's had planned since the beginning of time.

"For I know the plans I have for you," declares the LORD, "plans to prosper you and not to harm you, plans to give you hope and a future.
—Jeremiah 29:11 (NIV)

We can't always see those plans, and that's why life as a follower of Christ is an adventure. Even if we suffer through difficulties, He surprises us with good things.

You can stay all gloom and doom, waiting for the next bad thing to happen, or you can accept that you're in a rough place but it's not permanent. There is good at the end of your tunnel. There is promise for hope and future with God. Do not look back, do not stay stuck, but "keep your eyes focused and clear" so you can begin to see the future opportunities God has for you.

Today: Don't look back. Find one good thing in your day, and believe God has something better ahead. Even if you can't see it yet, begin to expect it!

• • • • • •

Jenna came to a retreat broken. Her ex-husband had just burned all of her clothes. She came with only the clothes on her back, expecting nothing, but looking for hope. The first thing she encountered was women who cared about her, then she found a room full of clothes for her to choose from. These clothes had been collected and organized for this single moms event. They were all new or almost new items, including shoes, dress and casual clothes, new underwear, and accessories. She was able to rebuild a wardrobe so she could work and live. It was all given to her. She arrived empty, defeated, and angry, expecting nothing for her tomorrows. But she went home with love in her heart, clothes for her body, hope, and expectation. While the enemy tries to steal our hope every day, God's Word and His people continuously offer us hope.

Hope for Transportation — *Try It*

My child, don't lose sight of common sense and discernment. Hang on to them, for they will refresh your soul. They are like jewels on a necklace. They keep you safe on your way, and your feet will not stumble. —Proverbs 3:21–23 (NLT)

This may seem like an odd thing to have hope for, but many moms struggle to find good and safe transportation for themselves and their children. If you need transportation, pray. God can do the miraculous!

Transportation is important. It gets us to work and our kids to school and everyone to social activities. If you live far from public transportation, you need a car. If you live in the city, you need safe transportation. This is not a surprise to God.

If you rely on public transportation, pray for safety and friendships so you're not traveling alone. Have your change or pass prepared so you can enter and exit without drama. Be aware of your surroundings, be wise, and be watchful.

If you need a car, ask God to provide one. But also prepare to purchase a car when the opportunity comes along by saving and building good credit.

God provides in many ways. I can't tell you how many single moms have been given a car or offered a car way below its value. When you're faithful to God, He's faithful to you. But don't just wait around for a free car, plan for your purchase. Begin to hope for a good, running car that will meet your needs.

Today: If you or your kids need a ride, pray for God's miraculous provision and protection. Pray daily, pray fervently, pray believing He will answer. And put some money aside today as seed money toward that car.

• • • • • •

When I had no car, my pastor said he had a car that didn't work sitting in his driveway. He went out to start it, and it ran, so he brought it to me to use as long as it lasted. It ran every day and every time I needed it. Many months later, when I was able to purchase a cheap car of my own, I returned his car. It never started again, and he had to junk it. But notice I had pursued buying a car of my own—I didn't just wait for this car to die, as it surely would, and leave me stranded. I continued to pray for a good car of my own, and God brought a car I could afford.

Hope for Wisdom — *Learn It*

In the same way, wisdom is sweet to your soul. If you find it, you will have a bright future, and your hopes will not be cut short. —Proverbs 24:14 (NLT)

Get all the advice and instruction you can, so you will be wise the rest of your life. —Proverbs 19:20 (NLT)

If you need wisdom, ask our generous God, and he will give it to you. He will not rebuke you for asking. —James 1:5 (NLT)

We live in a day and age where we need all the wisdom we can find in order to raise our families and succeed in life. But wisdom won't fall from the sky—we must seek it.

Do not be satisfied with little knowledge. Further your education as much as possible. If education is not possible, read, study, learn, and grow at your local library or through online reading.

Wisdom also comes from people, not just books. Begin to observe people who are successful in the areas you want to succeed (parenting, career, self-discipline, temperament, etc.). Watch and learn and look for mentors at your church or in your workplace.

There are many scriptures about gaining wisdom because it causes us to live godly and fulfilled lives. Don't put off gaining wisdom in an area where you're lacking.

Today: Ask yourself where you need to gain wisdom, and from whom you could gain this wisdom. Make an appointment to meet with that person and ask for their mentoring in this area. If they're unable to help, keep seeking. God will provide the right person at the right time for you to learn from. Set a time to research books that will guide you, either online or at your local library.

• • • • • •

Marla wanted a mentor for her job. She asked someone she trusted and that person said yes, but then her mentor had to change jobs and back out of her commitment. Marla pouted for a long time, felt rejected by this person, and refused to ask anyone else. A year later, she decided to ask another person to help her. This person was the perfect match. It's sad that Marla wasted over a year feeling sorry for herself, but it's good that she ultimately sought help. She ended up following the career path she'd hoped for because of what she learned from her mentor. Don't give up or feel rejected—keep seeking a mentor and God will provide the right person(s).

30
Day

Hope for Victory — *Rehearse It*

He will say to them, "Listen to me, all you men of Israel! Do not be afraid as you go out to fight your enemies today! Do not lose heart or panic or tremble before them. For the LORD your God is going with you! He will fight for you against your enemies, and he will give you victory!"
—Deuteronomy 20:3–4 (NLT)

You may feel defeated today, but God wants you to know the victory is in Him. Don't give up, lose heart, or panic. Trust in Him to bring you victory. This isn't easy to do when you're facing a giant of a problem, but if you've done all you know to do, it's time to rest in Him.

Your servant has killed both the lion and the bear; this uncircumcised Philistine will be like one of them, because he has defied the armies of the living God. The LORD who rescued me from the paw of the lion and the paw of the bear will rescue me from the hand of this Philistine. —1 Samuel 17:36–37 (NIV)

In this chapter, David faces Goliath, a giant of a man who threatened the entire nation of Israel. Nobody had nerve enough to face Goliath until a teenage shepherd boy named David came along. When Goliath spoke against God, David rallied. David rehearsed the past victories God had given him to build his faith. David knew he could not defeat this giant on his own—his hope was in God to give him another victory.

If you're in need of a victory, remember these words: *For the LORD your God is going with you! He will fight for you against your enemies, and he will give you victory!* —Deuteronomy 20:4 (NLT)

Today: Can you think of even one victory (or more) God has given you since you became a believer? Rehearse your victories, expect God to bring victory and believe in His power, not yours. Do all you can to prepare, then trust in Him for the results.

• • • • • •

Susan had lost hope of ever winning a court battle against her husband, who continuously brought her to court. He seemed to win despite affidavits of his behaviors, drinking, DUIs, and the fear of him his kids expressed. Susan felt very defeated. It took a long time for her victory, but it finally came! She was awarded the house, he was denied the alimony he requested, and the kids were finally freed from forced visitation.

Our timing is not always God's timing, but He will bring us the victory as we stand strong in our faith.

Personal goals:

Personal scriptures to memorize:

Notes: